DIGITAL ASSET MANAGEMENT: PLANNING FOR DEPLOYMENT

2nd Edition

An overview for organizations preparing for the deployment of a Digital Asset Management Application

By Ed Engman

Consultant - Hart Talbot

www.harttalbot.com

Contents

PART 1: WHAT IS DIGITAL ASSET MANAGEMENT?

INTRODUCTION

The book will provide helpful information for an organization preparing for the deployment of a Digital Asset Management application. The assumption is that the organization has at this point considered the benefits of digital asset sharing and is planning next steps for deployment.

The book is targeted for a business team or a project team that has responsibility for analysis and implementation. The book covers the following topics:

- Define Digital Asset Management
- Describe the core and optional functionality of a DAM application
- Discuss the role of metadata
- Look at different types of DAM Application Software
- Review the architectural requirements for supporting a DAM application
- Plan for deployment
- Describe required organizational processes

Although we discuss technology and functionality, this is not an analysis of DAM application products; the technology is moving too quickly to be able to talk about best-in-class at any given point in time. That said, it is still advised that the organization "dive-in" and not wait for the functionality of the future; the savings gained through activities like asset sharing makes adopting the technology too compelling to delay.

The key point is that the deployment of a Digital Asset Management application is more than the installation of software. The organization needs to plan and deploy the structure and support critical to the ongoing success of this important tool.

WHAT IS DIGITAL ASSET MANAGEMENT?

Digital Asset Management (DAM) is a term that describes the storage and distribution of digital assets. Digital assets are the electronic assets that a person or an organization owns. These assets could be images taken with a digital camera, scanned images in digital format, office documents like Word or Excel files, digital video, computer aided design (CAD) files, layout files, even entire web sites.

What DAM is *not* is *raw data* storage: granular data items like names, addresses, payroll records, account numbers and birth dates. These items are components of other business records and processes and should be managed using a database management system (DBMS) like Oracle, Microsoft SQL Server, or MySQL.

DAM is also not Content Management. A Content Management System (or CMS) is software that facilitates the update of content on a website. CMS utilizes software "templates"; essentially pages that are divided into components. Certain types of content, like comments or videos, can be displayed and easily updated within these components.

The term *Digital Asset Management* is interpreted as a software application, but it is broader than that; it is as much a verb as a noun. A Digital Asset Management *application* is computer software that enables the storage and distribution of digital assets.

Benefits:

Asset Re-use

Acme Company has offices around the globe. Marketing ads are developed in one country and stored in the DAM application. Acme employees in another country search for ads from within the DAM application, download the ads, and localize the ads for their own market needs.

Archival

Midwestern University produces over three hundred articles for academic publication per year. Once an article has been published, the author submits it to the records team at the university. The records team stores the file in the DAM application. Others can now search for the asset for their research.

E-Commerce

A photographer wants to sell photos to customers over the Internet. The photographer stores the digital images in a DAM application. Descriptive information about each image ("sunflower", "New York skyline") is added so that a customer can search for a specific subject and find relevant images. After the customer selects a specific asset and pays for it, they can download the asset directly from the site to their computer.

DAM as "Back-end" to Other Applications

The DAM application itself can function as a back end for other systems, providing content for other applications like a web site. If the web site uses a Content Management System or CMS (like Word Press) the web page can "call" a digital asset from a DAM application and display it. To display a different image the following week, the call is modified, but there is no need to move assets around (if they are in the DAM application). Requirements like performance and security need to be considered.

CORE FUNCTIONALITY AND OPTIONAL FUNCTIONALITY

CORE FUNCTIONALITY

There are two types of functionalities in a DAM application: core functionality – the essential functionality that the application requires, and optional functionality – good stuff, but not required. We will examine the core functionality first.

DAM application users search for and download assets. Let's say, for example, that a user is looking for an image of a sunflower for a marketing campaign. The user logs into the DAM application and searches using the term "sunflower". The results returned are reviewed (thumbnail images of the assets). The user selects the appropriate "sunflower" asset, and then downloads the asset to their personal computer.

In order to facilitate this process, the application must provide the appropriate tools to search for the asset, ways to display the asset for selection, and methods for downloading the asset. Here are the three key functions of a DAM:

- Search
- Display
- Download

SEARCH

"Search" is a term most users understand, particularly if they have used websites like Google. This is the fundamental function of a DAM: the ability for a user to find an asset by searching for some characteristic of the asset. For example, if the user searches the DAM application using the string "Sunflower", the application should return assets that contain Sunflowers. If this function doesn't work, the application is worthless. Imagine going to a card catalogue in a library and discovering that the book is in some other location than the one described on the index card. The importance of this function cannot be overstated. To provide the best search functionality, the DAM application must anticipate the search request of the user -- depending on the situation – and anticipate how much the user knows about the asset (maybe a little, maybe very little). In other words, it must provide the best results given the limited knowledge of the user.

We can divide search functionality in the following four categories:

SIMPLE SEARCH

Most users know how the functionality of a simple search works; the best example is the Internet Search Site *Google.com*. The user types a word or phrase into the search box and the site delivers a list of results. Fewer results are returned when more search terms are added (compare the number of results from a search for "dog" to the results of a search for "Pedigreed Saint Bernard Breeders in New England"). The DAM simple search works the same way. If the specific name of the asset is known, the user can type that in and (hopefully) receive one or two results. However, if the only piece of information known is that the asset was created in a specific year, and the user types the year in the search box, the results may be overwhelming. Again, users can continue to add specificity to the search to narrow down the number of results.

Although it is expected that the DAM application can do the search, the search is totally dependent on asset "metadata". Metadata is a term for data that describes other data and is *added by the organization*. There is no magic to this.

In DAM language, metadata describes either the content of the asset (description, category) or the properties of the asset (size, file type, date loaded to DAM, asset owner). When a user searches, they search the asset metadata. For the most part, metadata is added manually when the asset is ingested (uploaded) into the application. Therefore, the quality of the search results is dependent on the accuracy of the metadata (more on that in the next section).

Metadata is defined in "value pairs": field *names* and field *values*. For example, "File Size" is a metadata field name, and "25.6 MB" is a metadata field value. Here are additional examples:

Field Name	Field Value
Size	25.6 MB
Location	Exterior
Year	2023
Type	Image
Title	Sunflower

Usually, a simple search scans each of the metadata field *values* associated with an asset. When a match is found, a result is returned. By default, if multiple terms are entered in the simple search, the DAM application will perform an "AND" search (discussed later).

Let's look at how the following assets would be found in a simple search.

Title	Asset A	Asset B	Asset C
Size	25.6 MB	38.9 MB	15 KB
Location	Exterior	Interior	Interior
Year	2023	2023	2025
Type	Image	Video	Image
Subject	Sunflower	Flower Vase	Florist Store Interior 2023

The user types in **2025** in the simple search field:
Returns only Asset C

User types in **interior**
Returns Assets B and C

User types in **flower**

Returns assets A and B (Maybe! It depends on whether your search capability includes a substring search; that is, would it find the "flower" part of "Sunflower"? Sometimes this is an option the user can set. It is important to know how your DAM application executes this search. Depending on the configuration of the specific DAM application simple search it may find A and B, B only, or neither!).

ADVANCED SEARCH

Advanced Search takes search to the next level by offering the user the ability to search on specific metadata, using the value pairs described above. That is, the user can search for assets by looking for a value in one or more of the metadata fields. If there are thirty metadata fields related to each asset, the advanced search might offer thirty fields in which to search. Let's say the Advanced Search offers the fields described in the previous example. The user can select only the value pairs that they know. For example, the user knows the file was created in 2023. In the "Year" field, the user types in 2023.

Size

Location

Year   **2023**

Type

Title

In this example, Assets A and B are returned. Asset C is *not* returned, because **2023** does not appear in the YEAR field (it appears only in the *Title* Field of Asset C).

The user can also search more than one field. By default, searching with multiple fields uses an "AND" Search.

AND Searches. An "AND" search requires that each search term requested MUST be met. By default, most "complex" searches (search using more than one field) are "AND" searches, not "OR" searches. Hopefully, the DAM offers both "AND" and "OR" search capability.

In the following example, to narrow down the search the user might add a value for *Type*:

Size
Location
Year   **2023**
Type   **Image**
Title

In this case, only Asset A is returned, because it meets both criteria.   It is Year = 2023 **AND** Type = Image.

OR Searches. An "OR" search will return results if it meets ANY of the criteria listed. For example, if the previous search was done using Year "OR" Type, Assets A, B, and C would be returned: A and C would be returned because the *Type* for both assets is **Image**, and Assets A and B would be returned because both *Year* values are **2023**.

The user has the option of continuing to add values to narrow down a search.

It's also good to know if the DAM offers additional search "operators". An operator is simply how the values are compared. Here are examples of standard operators:

EQUALS: Straightforward; the value entered in the search equals the value in the metadata: Year = 2023

DOES NOT EQUAL: The value entered in the search does not equal the value of the metadata. For example, return all assets whose YEAR *does not* equal 2023. (This would return only Asset C).

CONTAINS: A "Substring" search, returns the asset if the value in the search matches a part or all of the metadata. For example,

Size

Location

Year

Type

Title CONTAINS "Store"

...would return Asset C. "Store" is a substring contained in that value.

DOES NOT CONTAIN: Just the opposite of CONTAINS, the substring does not appear in metadata.

GREATER THAN / LESS THAN: These are helpful searches if you are looking for files that are above or below a certain size, or perhaps created before or after a certain date.

Size   GREATER THAN **10MB**

Location

Year

Type

Title

In this example, the search would return assets A and B

Size

Location

Year   LESS THAN   **2025**

Type

Title

In this example, the search would return assets A and B

TREE SEARCH

Provided the user knows where to start, a Tree Search -- also known as "drill down" search -- provides the user the ability to refine a search by progressively selecting available options through a branch of folders. The user starts at the "root" of the tree, and then continues to select options until they get to a level that will return a workable number of assets.

Some DAM applications provide the user with a way to create their own tree searches. In the following example, we have created a custom tree with a root of YEAR, followed by TYPE, followed by LOCATION. The "+" to the left of the metadata field indicates that a level exists below. When no "+" appears, you have reached the end of that branch. Here is the "root" level; only 2023 and 2025 appear as they are the only years that appear in our metadata:

+2023
+2025

Now, let's expand (drill down) each of the options to see what further information is available:

+2023
        +Image
        +Video

+2025
        +Image

(Note: there are no 2025 "Video" assets).

Let's drill down to the next level:

+2023

    +Image

        Exterior

    +Video

        Interior

+2025

    +Image

        Interior

As you drill further down the branch, the further you narrow your search - - progressively fewer results will be displayed. For example, if you just clicked on "2023", you would receive two results. (A and B). But if you selected "2023" and "Image", you would receive one result (A). If built properly, this type of search can help users find an asset using information that they do know.

CONTENT SEARCH

Another search option available on some applications is the ability to search for text *inside* of an asset, like a word or phrase in a Microsoft Word or PDF document. This requires that your DAM indexes assets on a regular basis.[1] After being indexed, the content within the asset is available for search. For example, Asset D is a contract created using Microsoft Word. The contract contains the term "litigation". If the user types "litigation" in the Content Search box, Asset D would be returned in the result.

---

[1] "Indexing" is a database management term which means that the document text is cut up into small strings and stored in a database. Once a string is submitted via a content search, the database is searched for string matches, and the corresponding assets are returned.

This functionality would not work on images or videos (it can, but it's too complicated to discuss here), but works on Office documents, PDF files – any file whose text can be searched.

When reviewing potential DAM applications for your organization, it's important to understand the variety of searches available.

Asset "Sourcing"

The term asset sourcing refers to the process of locating an asset. For example, a user may contact the DAM support team to find an asset that they need. A search begins, usually within the DAM.

When assets can't be located within the DAM, a broader search takes place. It is helpful for the user to provide additional information: How do they know about the asset's existence? Did they find the asset on a company website?

COLLECTIONS

Most DAM applications offer the capability of grouping assets into "collections". For the purpose of search, these are user-created file folders which, when accessed by a link or some other affordance, displays a pre-selected group of assets.[2] Collections pre-empt the user from having to search for assets; someone has already done the work. For example, User A has searched the DAM application and discovered 15 assets relevant to Sunflowers. Of those 15, User A has determined that 12 can be used in her market. She groups these assets together in a collection called "Market Sunflower Images". A link to the collection is automatically posted on a page of collection links. She sends an email to User B letting him know she has created a collection in the DAM application called "Market Sunflower Images". User B logs into the DAM application and clicks on the appropriate collection link. The DAM application returns the 12 images, and User B then downloads the assets he needs.

---

[2] DAM vendors prefer the use of the term "Collection" or "Catalog" to "Folder". When a folder is deleted, the content within the folder is deleted as well. In a "collection" the collection may be deleted, but the assets still remain in the DAM application. Also, when an asset is modified, every collection containing the asset will automatically store the modified asset (it is, in fact, the same asset). In a folder, only the asset stored within the specific folder is modified.

RESULTS DISPLAY

After the search has been executed, the DAM will return / display the results. Ideally the results will be displayed in a preview format to allow the user to view the assets. The characteristics of the results display include:

- Format of the result
  - Size of thumbnail
  - Text only (no thumbnail)
- Number of results to return per page
- Order in which the results are displayed
- Corresponding metadata
- LIMIT on the number of results to return

Below is a sample page of results.

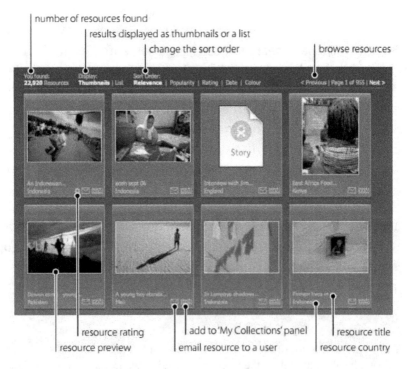

(courtesy resourcespace.org)

The thumbnail preview allows the user to view and compare the results from the search. DAM applications are becoming more sophisticated, and preview capability is being pushed by technology advances; more and better information can be crammed into the thumbnail real estate. Also, several DAM applications now allow users to alter the size of the result thumbnail, so that it can appear smaller or larger on the results page. There is a trade-off: the larger the thumbnail image, the fewer the number of results that can fit on a page. The user may want to see more thumbnails per page; this means the user doesn't have to move from page to page as frequently, but the load of images to the page may take longer. Thumbnails for videos may display a still image from within the video (or several). Zip files may display smaller thumbnails of the compressed assets within the file.

The user sees a thumbnail preview of each asset, relevant metadata for each asset, and the order (for example, by filename in alphabetic order) in which the assets appear. Depending on the flexibility of the application, the user may decide to view the results in some other order, like by date created or by largest size. The user may even want to see the results without the thumbnails!

To avoid unnecessary computer processing time, some DAM applications limit the number of results returned, or display some results, then prompt the user to view more by selecting a link, or by paging forward. For example, a user types in a search term (like the letter "a") that returns 200,000 responses. The application might limit the number of items returned to 10,000, and then prompt the user to click a link to see more.

Previews

Thumbnails don't always provide the level of detail required for the user to determine whether to download an asset, so usually a preview (a larger view of the asset) is launched by clicking a link near the thumbnail or clicking on the thumbnail itself.

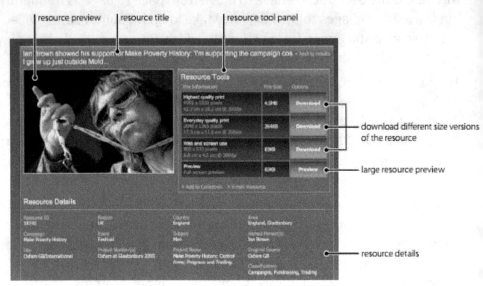

(courtesy: respourcespace.org)

For assets other than images, displaying the preview poses a challenge, because the software required to display specific assets may be "proprietary". For example, only Adobe InDesign is licensed to display a layout file created using Adobe InDesign software. However, available open-source programs have been developed to provide a view of these assets, and DAM application developers have integrated this capability in their products. In fact, these programs continue to evolve and provide better, more sophisticated previews. Resource Space, an open-source DAM application, offers previews for over two hundred types of digital files!

Previews for Popular File Types

Images

This is straightforward; the preview is a larger, better resolution version of the thumbnail image

CAD Files

Assets created in Computer Aided Design (CAD) files (like files created using AutoCAD) can't be displayed fully in previews, but an abstraction of the asset can be displayed.

Edited Images

Assets created in image editing software like Adobe Photoshop, display similar to image display.

Layouts

Layouts created in desktop publishing software like Adobe InDesign display like images or office documents.

GIF Files / Ads

Depending on the DAM application, these assets may display statically or with animation, as it would appear in a browser.

Office Documents

Some DAM applications allow you to page through a word document, spread sheet or PDF.

Videos

Video previews should be able to play the video. There are alternate ways to display the video; several DAM applications leverage software configured on the user's desktop PC; others can convert the video format to another video format during ingest.

DOWNLOAD AND EXTERNAL LINKS

It is assumed that once a user views the results, they will want to download one (or several) of the assets. Therefore, the instructions for downloading an asset should be obvious.

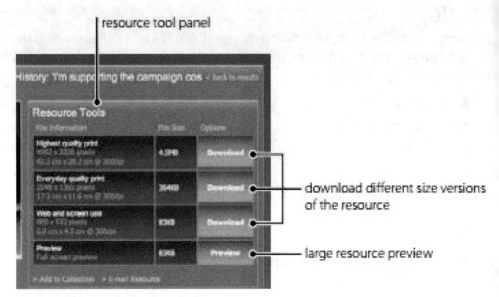

(courtesy resourcespace.org)

Depending on the DAM application, the user selects one or more objects for download. Some DAM applications require that the user move the asset into a shopping cart before downloading (particularly if the user is going to pay for the asset. However, most DAM shopping carts DO NOT infer a cost for downloading. The shopping cart simply holds a group of assets until the user is ready to download). In other applications, the user may be offered several options, including a direct download of a single asset from the thumbnail, or a direct download from the asset preview.

Once a user initiates the process for downloading, the DAM application goes into action. If the user requests a small .jpg file, the DAM may just send it as is. However, depending on the asset size (or the number of assets in the download), the DAM application may compress (or "zip") the file before download. This is done to save time during the file transfer process. When the user receives the downloaded file on their personal computer, they will need to un-compress (or unzip) the file using a utility tool appropriate for the target operating system.

Sending an "External Link"

In some DAM applications, the user can send an asset to an external user, that is, to someone who does not have access to the DAM application. The external user receives an email with a download link, initiates the transfer by clicking on the link, and then waits while the file is transferred to them. The link forwarder (the DAM application user) takes responsibility for the asset transfer, ensuring the receiver has appropriate authorization to use the asset. The DAM application usually maintains an audit trail of the external link activity, and can identify the link forwarder, if needed.

UPLOAD (INGEST)

Uploading or "ingesting" assets is the process of loading the asset into the DAM application. Because of security, ingest is not a function granted to most users. The term "ingest" is preferred to the term "upload" because you are doing more than posting a file; you are in essence "feeding" the asset to the application.

There are two models of ingesting assets: Centralized and Distributed.

Centralized

Early DAM applications restricted the ingest capability to a few users because the ability to add metadata was, at that point, primitive functionality. Asset owners transferred their assets to a team or person (by File Transfer Protocol – FTP – or even email) along with the relevant asset metadata. The librarian then ingested the assets into the DAM application. The process requires two file transfers (to the librarian and then to the application) and is bulky and slow.

Distributed

As DAM applications matured, form improvements -- like drop-down fields and the designation of fields as "mandatory" or "optional" -- facilitated "self-serve" ingesting. However, this model brought with it its own set of problems, including metadata quality issues.

There are also variations of the distributed model, where small teams of librarians are located in various geographic regions, or one librarian is employed by each company storing assets in the DAM application.

Below is a list of advantages and disadvantages for the two models. Keep in mind that whichever model is chosen, there still needs to be a business support team (help desk).

Activity	Central	Distributed
Ingest process	Requires at least two file transfer stages and can result in lost assets or assets traveling through unsecure channels.	Quick; as fast as the asset owner can ingest.
Metadata Quality	Metadata quality is best maintained when a few librarians are ingesting assets. DAM librarians develop experience and intimacy with assets and provide a level of consistency when adding the metadata.	Distributed proponents will tell you that metadata quality can be enforced by deploying controlled form fields. Forcing users to enter data in mandatory fields is one technique, as is the use of drop-down fields which requires the user to select among given options. However, providing "free-form" metadata text fields creates metadata quality issues.
Asset Sourcing	As the central point of asset ingesting, librarians know what assets are in the DAM, and who supplied them with the assets. As a result, sourcing becomes relatively easy.	Asset owners are intimate with their own assets but can't provide much help regarding other assets. A culture of not coordinating activity leads to difficult asset sourcing.
Asset Rights	Central librarians should have some knowledge about asset rights, but not as much knowledge as the asset owner. Would be able to locate the asset owner quickly, however.	Asset owners are intimate with their own assets and can provide usage information quickly. Locating the asset owner may be difficult.
Application Support	Application support will be required anyway, so the librarian and support function could be combined.	Doesn't take advantage of resources that may be required for application support.

THE INGEST PROCESS

The process for asset ingests is not too dissimilar from DAM application to DAM application. While working within the application, the librarian locates and selects the asset on their computer. The librarian then either clicks a button to begin the ingest process, or the ingest process starts automatically. The DAM application first displays a form which requires the librarian to enter descriptive metadata (additional metadata will be pulled automatically by the DAM application, for example, *Date Ingested*).

Most DAM applications offer a variety of methods to ingest an asset. Here is a list of the some of the ingest capabilities:

"Ingest File" Dialog Box: Click on the box and navigate to the location where the asset is stored on your computer

Drag and Drop: Click and drag the asset to some area on the DAM application

Multiple Asset Ingest: One of the more powerful features of a DAM application is the ability to ingest more than one asset at a time. Consider the task of having to ingest five hundred individual frames from an animation! (Of course, these could always be zipped and then ingested in one file!). Most DAM applications allow you to ingest multiple assets concurrently, and then provide the ability to alter the metadata for each asset individually after the ingest.

Sticky Data: Sticky data refers to data that remains in the metadata form fields after an ingest. When the user logs in next time (which could be several weeks later), the metadata used in the last upload is already present in the form fields; only a few individual fields (like *Title*) may need to be updated.

Templates: A template is a pre-populated metadata form. If a specific type of asset is loaded over an extended period of time, the librarian may want to save the data in the form as a template. In the future, when the asset type is being prepared for ingest, the librarian will select a template and the metadata form will pre-populate with the appropriate data.

Mass Update / Edit: At some point, there may be several assets that need to be updated with new information. For example, say that supplier "Company A" has been bought by "Company B", and you want to update all assets that contain Company A to say Company B. You can search for all assets with supplier as Company A, select all the assets, click on a "mass update" button or link, and be prompted with a generic metadata form. The new metadata entered in the generic mass update form will update the appropriate field for all the selected assets.

Sample Metadata Form

The librarian may be prompted with a form like this:

Identifier	
Subject	[ ]
Title	[ ]
Filename	sunflower18.jpg
Description	[ ]
Location	[ ]
Color	
Resolution Options	
Status	
Market Usage	[ ]
Price	[ ]
Keywords	[ ]
Type	
Format	jpg
Date Uplaoded	12/24/2012
Size	2.34 MB
Photographer	[ ]
Publisher	ajones01

[Submit]

The technical metadata fields were populated when the asset was selected. The *identifier* will be populated once the Submit button is clicked,

and the information is committed to the database.

Here is the form prior to the "submit". The *Color, Resolution Options, Status*, and *Type* fields were selected from Drop Down menus.

Identifier

Subject   Sunflower

Title   Sunflower Image 18

Filename   sunflower18.jpg

Description   Outdoor image of Sunflower. Vernmont shoot
                 Part of Flower Series 20A

Location   Vermont

Color   Color

Resolution Options   Highest

Status   Public

Market Usage   USA, CAN

Price $450.00

Keywords   Sunflower, flower, field, flora, Vermont,
                 outdoors, medium shot, exterior, nature

Type   Image

Format   jpg

Date Uplaoded   12/24/2012

Size   2.34 MB

Photographer   Wilson

Publisher   ajones01

Submit

ACCESS AND SECURITY

Access is a key function in a DAM application. Security controls must be understood to ensure that only users that are allowed to view and download an asset have that capability. Assets are usually protected in two ways:

- Security based on user role
- Security based on asset metadata

Security Based on User Role

When planning for the deployment of a DAM application, the project team will develop a set of roles that have specific access. For example, they will likely create one role that allows users to only view or read assets, another role to read and download assets, another role to read, download and ingest assets, etc. A user given "read only" access can peruse the assets within the DAM application but does not have the authority to download the assets; to download, they must contact another user or a system administrator.

The project team or business team will develop a role / access matrix for the DAM application. The user role is defined in the first column; the DAM application functionality is defined in the first row. Below is a simple example.

Role	Read	Download	Ingest	Make Private	Private Read	Delete
Read (R)	X					
Read and Download (RD)	X	X				
Read, Download, and Ingest (RDI)	X	X	X	X		
Administrator (A)	X	X	X	X	X	X

The organization then determines which type of business users fit which roles. The number of administrators is usually low (like two or three), because of the ability to perform powerful functions like asset deletion.

Here is an example of how the roles may be distributed in an organization.

Name (user ID)	Department	Role
Allan	Engineering	R (Read only)
Betty	Engineering	RDI (Read, Download and Ingest)
Charles	Production	RD (Read and Download)
David	Administration	A (Administrator)

In this example, Allan can only read assets; he can't download them. Betty, Charles and David can read and download assets. Betty and David can ingest assets. Only David can delete assets.

Security Based on Asset (Using Asset Metadata)

Another way to maintain security is to protect the asset at the metadata level. This means that the information contained in a metadata value field will control asset usage.

Assets can also be secured by a user characteristic. For example, only users in Brazil are allowed to see a specific set of assets.

Here is another example which demonstrates how the user's organization is used to determine which assets are viewable. The table shows us that users aligned to the *Development* department have access to assets whose Asset Status (metadata field) is equal to Engineering, Production, or Test (metadata field value):

Department	Asset Status					
	Prototype	Engineering	Production	Test	Launch	Archive
Engineering	X	X				
Development		X	X	X		
Production		X	X	X	X	
Administration	X	X	X	X	X	X

The application examines the department aligned to the user ID.

In the table below, we note that Charles is in the Production department. According to the above table, Charles can read and download assets whose *Asset Status* is Engineering, Production or Test (but Charles can't ingest or delete assets – note that his role code is RD). Allan can only read assets whose *Asset Status* is Prototype or Engineering but can't download *any* assets (because of his "R" status).

Name (user ID)	Department	Role
Allan	Engineering	R
Betty	Engineering	RDI
Charles	Production	RD
David	Administration	A

Another metadata field that could be used to restrict access is a "private" user field, where the asset is restricted to only those user ID's that are specifically entered in the field. For example, Betty ingests an Engineering asset, but in the *Private User* Field adds only the name *Allan*. Even though Charles can see Engineering assets, this particular asset has been restricted only to Allan (who can only read the file). Note, however, that David can also see the file (the "Administrator" role can read all *Private User* assets).

Private Assets

Private assets are assets that only certain users are allowed to read and download (there may be security reasons why the asset is protected from other users). Depending on the DAM application or the business need, the term could be "Private", "Protected", "Secured", "Confidential", or something else; the treatment of the asset is the same (not for public display!).

After receiving the search results, the user may expect to see many more assets than those displayed, but the DAM application restricts the display of private assets (and of course, their download). Some DAM applications will inform the user that only certain assets returned from the search can be displayed (for example, "Displaying 42 of 114 assets"). This lets the user know that there are more assets available, but they are only allowed to view a subset (the non-private assets).

Leveraging Existing Security Infrastructure

Over the course of the last decade, organizations have implemented special technologies to reduce the number of logon ID's and passwords required to access company applications. It is desirable that the DAM application you are deploying has "hooks" or application programming interfaces (API's) that enable the integration of the DAM application with the company security infrastructure. This ability can add simplification to DAM security. For example, if the user leaves the company, their access to the DAM will be terminated automatically when their user account is deleted from the company access management system.

The project team should understand how the current security infrastructure can "talk" to the DAM application and leverage existing company user ID's and passwords.

RULES

Rules are provided by the DAM application to enforce business processes or audit requirements. In practical terms, they are likely to be small software programs that can be applied to the application based on user-defined criteria. For example, the business team deems that no user can download more than 10 assets per day. The "rule" counts the number of downloads per user, then prohibits further downloads after the limit is reached.

Depending on how your DAM application works, the rules may take the form of "SQL" statements that are automatically generated based on options you select.[3]

You should identify all the rules your organization will need when you develop your requirements.

---

[3] SQL stands for Structured Query Language and is the standard programming code for querying databases (regardless of database product).

AUDIT REQUIREMENTS

Large companies have audit requirements. These requirements can include:

- The life cycle of an asset; when an asset gets deleted, or when it gets archived
- The audit trail of a downloaded asset; who has downloaded an asset, or sent an external link?
- How often are user accounts deleted?
- Who deleted an asset?
- How often are assets backed-up?

If an organization is unsure of their audit requirements, the team should consult its finance and security departments.

Once the audit requirements are known, they must be integrated in the operational model of the application. For example, if an asset expires two years after its public posting, an automated or manual process must be put in place to ensure that the expired assets stored in the DAM application are treated according to the process. At "expiry" the image may need to be watermarked, moved to an archive status, or deleted. If no record retention policy exists, the deployment team should consider developing one.

Audit requirements will likely dictate how often the application, database, and folder structure are backed-up. A "back-up" is a copy of the application, metadata, and digital assets on "removable media" (like a DVD or portable hard drive), then moved offsite for safe storage.

Also, audit requirements may require proof of digital asset tracking.

REPORTING AND ANALYTICS

A function the DAM application must provide is robust reporting capability. The following reporting features should be standard:

- Number of users, active users, dormant users
- Number of assets, asset types
- Total asset size (capacity used)
- Number of downloads by user, by asset, by market, other

To meet this requirement, the vendor may create database "copies" (so that the processing required to generate the report doesn't impact application performance), or they may allow access directly to the database. Understand how reporting is actually done in the DAM application. For example, the vendor may only supply the data; it is the company's responsibility to write the queries or develop reports (using a third-party tool) from the data provided.

Analytics

Analytics differs somewhat from reporting: it deals with activity regarding the site itself, not the interaction between users and assets within the site. Analytics collects information like how long a user stays on the site, or on a specific page; which pages are visited most often, and which are visited least? What path of pages do the users follow? This type of data can help the team discover problem pages or help with the re-design of the process flow. Optimization testing, done in coordination with analytics, allows the company to tinker with page designs to better adjust the user experience. Depending on the agreement with the DAM application vendor, analytics could be the responsibility of the company, so ensure these duties are clear when negotiating. There are free tools (like Google Analytics) and there are commercial tools (like Omniture). Ensure whatever you select can support your deployment globally, in all markets.

OPTIONAL FUNCTIONALITY

DAM Application vendors offer much more functionality than the core features listed above. When evaluating DAM applications for use in your organization, you should determine how critical these additional functions are. Keep in mind that these functions add overhead to your deployment and testing processes and could become distractions that interfere with the core requirements of your organization. On the other hand, the additional functionality may be worth the investment:

Artificial Intelligence

These are services provided by companies like *Google Vision* or *Amazon Rekognition* that scan your images or documents and generate metadata automatically, potentially reducing manual metadata ingest. The software must be "trained" to identify the elements you wish to detect.

Asset Editing

Some DAM applications offer limited image or video edit capability. When evaluating DAM applications, determine if users will utilize this functionality. Most external image and video editor applications are more feature-rich and better suited for editing.

Asset Owner Notification / Rights Owner Notification

Some DAM applications offer the ability to contact an asset owner or rights owner directly. For example, the user can select an asset, and then click on a button or link to send a note to the ingest librarian or the rights owner.

Asset Tracking

Assets can also be invisibly "stamped" for security purposes, primarily to track the routing of an asset. Special image tracking technology (called steganography) is used to read images and determine origin. For example, a special code or pixel is inserted on the downloaded image that says User A downloaded this asset from DAM Application B on a certain date. This may be a requirement of your organization's audit process.

Check-in and Check-out

If the DAM application is going to be used for work-in-progress, Check-In / Check-out functionality is critical (the functionality is irrelevant if the DAM application is only storing finished assets). Check-in / Check-out ensures that only one version of the asset is being worked on at any point in time. For example, User A is told to make updates to Asset X, Version 1. User A "checks out" the asset from the DAM application. At this point, Asset X is still available for download but can't be checked-out for edit by other users (it is in "locked" status). After User A completes the edits, the asset is "checked-in" to the application, replacing the existing Asset X (it is now Asset X, Version 2). The "locked" status is removed, and the asset is available for follow-up edits. Downloaders of the previous Asset X may be notified that a new version of Asset X exists.

File Conversion

File conversion is probably the most popular option, and in some cases has become a standard feature of DAM applications. For example, the librarian may ingest a high-resolution image in TIFF format. Users then have the option of downloading it in the original TIFF format, or in another format other than TIFF, like JPG or GIF format. The conversion is executed by the DAM application prior to the download. The same conversion can apply to video assets; the user may want to download a smaller video file format simply to view or make rough edits.

Most DAM applications can provide a lower resolution of the original asset but can't create a higher resolution from a low resolution original (there are third party programs, however, that can "res up" an image).

Improved Ingest and Download Speed

One of the more gruelling tasks associated with librarian work is waiting for assets to ingest and download. It is often assumed that file transfer speed is something the business is "stuck" with, based on their existing network capability and the general Internet infrastructure available in their market. However, there are technologies available that will help improve transfer speed, the most popular of which is User Datagram Protocol (UDP). UDP is an alternative to Transmission Control Protocol over Internet Protocol (TCP/IP); it performs the same function, but because it does not do a packet check at the end of the transmission, it can transfer files at much higher speeds. There are a few vendors who currently provide a commercial UDP product (Aspera, Signiant), and there is an open source version available. Determine if your DAM application has this capability integrated. Slow processing speed is one of the reasons that users dislike downloading from a DAM application.

Messaging

Some DAM applications offer internal messaging, that is, sending messages from one user to another user (or users) *within* the application itself. Sometimes this is a valuable feature as users can be notified if assets are added, modified, or deleted. However, many DAM application can also do their messaging externally (using the user's email address) as important messages may go unread if the user has not logged in to the DAM application for a while.

Multilingual

Depending on the global scope of the application, the ability for the application to display information in languages other than English may be core functionality. Most major DAM applications feature at least the presentation of metadata in multiple languages, but this capability needs to be validated. Some packages feature right-to-left language capability as well.

Shopping Cart

The shopping cart is a virtual temporary storage area where assets are held until the user is ready to leave the system, at which point they may leave the assets in the shopping cart, download some or all of the assets, or pay for the assets. Most DAMs use the shopping cart as a metaphor; a place to hold assets temporarily. A Shopping Cart is not likely to infer that download users pay for assets.

User Alert

A user alert is a notification to the user on the home page or landing page of the DAM application. The purpose of the alert is to communicate information to the user: things like system availability, new functionality, or new processes. The key characteristic of this notification is that it should be available regardless of the availability of the DAM application; if the application is down, the alert will still be viewable by users (hopefully letting them know the application is not available!).

Version Restore

The administrator has the option to restore a previous version of an asset.

View and Mark-up

View and Mark-up is the process of identifying elements of an image; the elements suggest action on the asset that should be taken. A modest palette of drawing tools (like a circle tool) is supplied to the user to identify elements within the image. A window may pop-up to allow the user to explain the purpose of the action (for example, "remove this tree", or "color needs to be blue, not green"). The circle and notes are viewable by other users and follow-up action may be taken.

Watermark

This capability stamps a watermark on images (the capability is available for video, as well). Watermarking is applied to assets to ensure that rights are not being violated, or that asset accuracy cannot be guaranteed. The watermark may be applied during the view or during the download.

Zoom In

The DAM application may have a feature that allows the user to zoom-in within the asset.

METADATA

A critical component of a DAM application is the quality of the metadata. As we discussed earlier, metadata is integral to successful searching; the search is only as good as the metadata. Keep in mind that the metadata is "joined" to the asset at the point of ingest, manually entered by the librarian using a form within the DAM application. Metadata can be added, edited, and deleted after the asset is ingested into the DAM.

Here are items regarding metadata that will need to be discussed:

- Defining metadata fields
- How many metadata fields?
- What are the dependencies between metadata fields?
- How are the fields to be presented?
- Enforcing quality data entry

Process to Define Metadata

- Form a small group of representative asset owners to participate
- Start with a list of "standard" metadata
- Consider what terms users will use to find assets
- List terms and prioritize, trim list to a usable number of fields
- Vet with the stakeholders
- Develop a metadata schema
- Implement

DEFINING METADATA FIELDS

There are two types of metadata fields: descriptive and technical. Descriptive metadata describes the content within the asset. Technical metadata describes the physical properties of the asset itself. Though "invisible" to an end user, technical data accompanies a digital asset and includes information like the date the image was taken, the type of camera used, and the size of the asset. [4]

Below is an example of the "invisible" technical data that accompanies an image:

File size : 2315489 Bytes
MIME type : image/jpeg
Image size : 3648 x 2736
Camera make : Canon
Camera model : Canon PowerShot S95
Image timestamp : 2025:01:13 18:36:09
Image number : 109-0037
Exposure time : 1/20 s
Aperture : F2.8
Subject distance: 6553
Image quality : Fine
Exif Resolution : 3648 x 2736
White balance : Auto
Thumbnail : image/jpeg, 6834 Bytes

(data provided by http://www.exifviewer.org/)

For technical metadata fields, like file type, file size, and date created, the DAM application can pull the data directly from the file during ingest. Descriptive metadata needs to be added manually by the librarian at point of ingest.

---

[4] The technical data is either XMP (Extended Metadata Platform) or EXIF (Exchangeable Image File) data and is embedded in the image file. Special tools allow you to read this data, and these tools are integrated into DAM applications in order to move this data into a metadata field.

How do I go about determining what descriptive metadata fields I need?

Put yourself in the position of the user -- how would the user search for your assets? The answer will be different from company to company. For example, for a company selling stock images on a website, "Subject" is the most important metadata field. The first thing users want to do is find an image based on the subject, say "Sunflower" or "New York Skyline".

Once you have a solid list of search terms, sort the terms in order of priority. If your list is starting to grow beyond a reasonable number of metadata fields (say, forty), consider trimming some of the less important fields. When prioritizing, ask if the metadata applies to every asset. Also, how easy is it for the librarian to get the metadata? Does this metadata apply to every asset?

How Many Metadata Fields should we have?

The more complex your assets (the more file types, file varieties, user types, business teams supported) the more metadata fields you are likely to have. However, the more metadata fields you have, the more complicated the ingest process becomes: first, the opportunity for data entry error increases; second, the more fields in the ingest form, the more difficult and longer the ingest process takes to complete.

Is there an ideal number of metadata fields?

No. But best practices suggest the number should be low (less than forty). Although new DAM applications are highly configurable, resist the temptation to take full advantage of the functionality; keep in mind that these assets will need to be maintained, tested, and probably -- at some point in their lifecycle -- migrated to another application.

In this example, let's think about the metadata fields we want to include. The first may be "Subject".

Now let's answer some questions about the "Subject" metadata field:

- How big is it? (How many characters should it hold)?
- Does the field need to be filled in (Is this a mandatory field or an optional field?)
- Are we providing the values from a drop-down menu, or are users typing the data in directly?
- Is it text / date / numbers? Should we offer a data "mask" or pattern to ensure data is entered in a standard format (like a telephone number)?
- Is the appearance of this field dependent on data entered (or a selection made) from a previous field in the form?
- Can the field hold multiple values?

Asset Migration

While defining the metadata, another concept to keep in mind is where the assets are now; are they in an existing DAM application, or will they be coming off a share drive (or collection of share drives)? See the *Asset Migration* section for further details.

The "Dublin Core"

An additional source for metadata consideration is to examine the "Dublin Core". This is a set of metadata (targeted for web page use, mainly) agreed to by several standards organizations, and a good place to start.

(http://dublincore.org/documents/dces/)

CREATING A METADATA SCHEMA

Once we have identified the metadata fields, the next step is documenting them, and then adding relevant descriptive data. On the next page is a sample:

ID	Field Name	Type	Size / Characters	Manda-tory	Dependent on	Multi Val-ues	Drop-down values
1	Identifier	Text	AutoNum	System			
2	Subject	Text	40	Yes			
3	Description	Text	200	Yes			
4	Location	DD		Yes			Interior, Exterior, Other
5	Color	DD		Yes			Color, Black and White
6	Resolution Options	DD		Yes			Highest, Lowest
7	Asset Status	DD		Yes			Public, Private
8	Restricted Users	Text		Yes	Restriction = Private	Comma separated	
9	File Name	Text	64	System			
10	Rights Associated	Yes / No		Yes			
11	Rights Expiry Date	Date	xx/xx/xxxx	Yes	Rights Associated = Yes		
12	Rights Media Usage	DD	20	Yes	Rights Associated = Yes	Multiple can be selected	TVC, Print, Digital, In-store, Other
13	Rights Market Usage	Text	3	Yes	Rights Associated = Yes	Comma separated	
14	Title	Text	40	Yes			
15	Price	Number	$xxxxxxx.xx	Yes			
16	Keywords	Text	300	No		Comma separated	
17	Type	DD		Yes			Image, Video, Audio, Other
18	Video Type	DD		Yes	Type = Video		avi, wav, mp4, other
19	Format	Text	6	System			
20	Publisher	Text	30	System			
21	Date Ingested	Text	xx/xx/xxxx	System			
22	Photographer	Text	30	No			
23	Size	Text	10	System			

In this example we have defined 23 metadata fields.

Column Descriptions:

ID is just an arbitrary ID number we've assigned each metadata field

Field Name is the name of the metadata field as it will appear in the DAM application. Where feasible, we have used the Dublin Core terms for our metadata field names, but an organization has complete flexibility to use whatever names they want

Type is the field type; how the data will be entered into the form. "DD" stands for Drop Down

Size / Characters is the number of characters that will fit within the field OR the format of the field. AutoNum is a database term that means that the database management system automatically assigns a sequential number for every record added. For example, the first file ingested will be "1", the next one loaded "2", and so on.

Mandatory is whether the field MUST be completed when the asset is being ingested. "System" means that the information is being pulled directly by the application (this is a "Technical" metadata field); it is not manually entered in the metadata field.

Dependent on means that the field is not visible UNLESS the condition listed is met. For example, the "Restricted Users" field will not appear on the form unless the "Asset Status" field is "Private".

Multivalues means that the field can store more than one value. "Comma separated" indicates that each value entered will be separated with a comma.

Drop-down Values are the values that will appear when the field is clicked on.

Enforcing Data Quality: Form Control

The "quality" of the metadata is enforced at the point of ingest. For technical metadata, there is usually no concern (unless the technical data accompanying the image is corrupt, which happens), but for manually entered descriptive data, the opportunity for data entry error is significant.

To ensure quality, the amount of manual data entry should be reduced (particularly in a distributed ingest model), and this can be done by applying common form design techniques:

- Require that certain fields (mandatory fields) are filled-in
- Replace freeform text fields with drop-down lists forcing users to make a choice
- Hide fields that are dependent on values entered in previous fields. For example, don't expose the *video format* field if the *asset type* is not "video"
- Provide data "masks" that force the user to enter data using a specific format (like a date or a phone number)

In the above metadata schema example, most fields are indicated as mandatory, which means the DAM application will not ingest the asset unless these fields are completed. You'll also note that several of the metadata fields include dropdowns. A dropdown forces a user to select an option. This eliminates free-form data entry where typing mistakes can occur.

RIGHTS

Protecting asset rights is critical in the operation of a DAM application. An asset may be copyright protected by the photographer, or perhaps there are actors (talent) in the asset or doing the voiceover work. Sometimes rights are granted for certain markets and not others. Regardless of the specific rights, the DAM application must have the functionality to protect and enforce these rights.

To ensure your DAM application can protect these rights, first define the types of rights associated with each asset, and then understand how the business currently enforces these rights. Next, you should design your metadata and create download rules to ensure that these rights are protected.

Here is an example: Asset A is a video asset featuring two actors in the video itself and another actor doing voice over. According to their contracts, they are compensated only for digital usage in Market A, for one year following the initial release of the video (release date January 1, 2025). The contracts must be renewed by January 1, 2026, or the asset can no longer be used. The metadata should then include fields for media / channel usage (in this example, the selection would be digital only), market usage, and a rights expiry date.

When a user from Market B tries to download this asset, they should be prohibited from doing so; perhaps even receiving an alert explaining that the rights associated with the asset are only for Market A (the check can be made against the user's market, contained in their security profile). On January 10, 2025, a user from Market A attempts to download the asset, but is prohibited from doing so, receiving an alert that the talent rights for this specific asset have expired. Another user from Market A downloads the asset for television usage on 7/1/2025. In this case, nothing may protect the asset from this usage other than perhaps a general alert that there are rights associated with the asset. The user then needs to review the metadata to ensure the asset usage will comply. If not covered by a functional rule prohibiting the download, the company needs to understand its exposure to this risk.

CONFIGURING FORM FIELDS TO MANAGE RIGHTS

The following is an example of how form fields and metadata are defined to enforce company procedures. The translation of business rules into automated processes will take some effort, so allow adequate time for this development.

Example:
Downloaders of assets want two things: they want to find the right asset and, when found, they want to know if they have the rights to use it. Enforcing rights usage is a good example of how form fields, rules, and metadata work together. In our example, ABC Company has purchased the digital rights to an image (Asset "A") for use in the US and Canada and purchased the digital and print rights for Mexico. The rights were bought by Jane Doe on January 1, 2025.

The rights are owned for two years and expire on December 31, 2026. Media channel rights for each market may differ, but they all expire at the same time.

Asset	Rights Owner	Rights Expire	Market	Channel
"A"	rights@abcco.com	12/31/2026	USA	Digital
			Canada	Digital
			Mexico	Digital
			Mexico	Print
"B"	rights@abcco.com	3/1/2026	USA	Digital
			Canada	Digital

The design goal is to configure the metadata to ensure users understand the rights associated with the image before they download. The deployment team has written the following functional requirements for rights-protected assets:

ID	Description	Rationale	Test
210	The user may not download assets if rights have not been purchased for the user's market	Ensure that we are enforcing legal rights for asset usage	Users from markets not included in the rights purchase cannot download assets Users from markets *included* in the rights purchase *can* download assets
211	The user may not download assets whose rights have expired	Ensure that we are enforcing legal rights for asset usage	Users cannot download rights-expired assets Users can download rights-protected assets whose expiry date has not been reached.
212	The user may not download assets for media usage if the rights for the specific usage channel have not been purchased	Ensure that we are enforcing legal rights for asset usage	Users are notified that the asset is for specific channel usage and agree that this is the channel in which they will be using the asset
212	The asset buyer responsible or asset buying team responsible for the rights should be identified in the application	If rights are not understood for the specific asset, users may contact the buyer / team and inquire about rights usage	Users can contact the buyer / team successfully

To enforce these rights, the team determined that the following metadata fields need to be defined:

ID	Field Name	Type	Size / Characters	Manda-tory	Dependent on	Multi Values	Drop-down values
10	Rights Associated	Yes / No		Yes			
11	Rights Expiry Date	Date	xx/xx/xxxx	Yes	Rights Associated = Yes		
12	Rights Market Us-age	Text (Re-peating)	3	Yes	Rights Associated = Yes		Popu-lated from market code list
13	Rights Media Us-age	Check Box (Re-peating)	20	Yes	Rights Associated = Yes	Multiple can be se-lected	TVC, Print, Dig-ital, In-store, Other
14	Rights Owner	Text	40	Yes	Rights Associated = Yes		

The deployment team has defined the metadata fields to work within the form as follows:

First, the form prompts the librarian to select whether the asset is rights-protected. (Of course, we are assuming that this information is known to the librarian. If it is not known, the design may need to be adjusted). If the asset is not rights-protected, the librarian will select "No." By selecting "No", the other four rights fields remain hidden. It is assumed that any asset marked "No" can be used in any market for any media usage.

If the librarian selects "Yes", the other four fields will appear. The first field that appears is *Rights Expiry Date*. Since this date applies to all markets and media channels for the same asset, the metadata value entered will apply to every market and market usage. The "Rights Owner" applies to all markets and usages as well. The company has determined that the best information to enter in the *Rights Owner* field is the email address for the Art Buying department (rights@abcco.com).

The librarian selects *USA* from the Rights Market Usage drop down field.

The Rights Media Usage field is also available and is represented by a series of check boxes; several media usage fields can be selected, if they apply. For USA, the librarian checks only "Digital". The librarian then selects the next market and its accompanying media usage and continues through the markets and usage channels until all markets are completed. If a market is not included in this list, it is assumed it does not have any rights to usage. Now that the rights have been identified, the DAM application enforces the rules. A user from Australia selects Asset "A" and clicks on the download button. An "alert" appears with a message:

> "The image you have selected for your download does not have rights for use in your market. If you are interested in extending these rights, please contact the Rights Owner."

The DAM application has used a "rule". In coding terms, they could not find a match between the user's market (contained in the user's security profile) and the markets that have rights to this asset. If the DAM application has the capability, perhaps an email link is provided in the alert that the user can click on in order to send a note to the Rights Owner. The market alert will be the first alert displayed because no further action will be taken if the market is not on the list.

Let's say that the user is from Mexico and wants to download an asset on October 1, 2025. The market "rule" is again invoked, and this time the DAM application allows the download to proceed. A second rule is also invoked: Is the download date within the rights date range? It is, therefore, the download will continue (otherwise, the next alert would appear).

But before the transfer is finalized, one more alert is presented to the user.

> "The rights for this asset are restricted to certain media channels. Please review the channels available. To extend the rights to a new media channel for this market, please contact the Rights Owner. To continue the download, please click "Submit". To terminate the download, click "Cancel."

Here's an issue. The company does not have an automated way to enforce media channel usage; once the asset is downloaded, the user will be able to apply the asset to any channel he or she wants. This leaves some expo-sure of risk to the company. The alert will mitigate the risk, but not elimi-nate it. The company needs to determine if this is acceptable.

If the DAM application has the ability to display metadata, the actual chan-nels for that market could be included in the alert.

> "This asset is approved for the following uses in your market: "<u>Dig-ital, Print</u>". To extend the rights to a different media usage for this market, please contact the Rights Owner.
> To continue the download, please click "Submit. To terminate the download, click "Cancel."

Again, this rule cannot enforce the ultimate usage; it's just a little more descriptive. Note that <u>Digital</u> and <u>Print</u> are underlined. If there were more channels, each would appear in this note.

In the test plan, conditions for each rule should be fully tested, both the situations that allow download and those that invoke alerts.

A note about the *Keywords* field

The Keywords field is a special field where librarians can store descriptive information about the asset. For example, for the "Sunflower" asset, key-words might include "flower", "field", "large flowers", "garden" – addi-tional words that assist in the search of the asset. In my experience, this field is always underutilized.

INFRASTRUCTURE

Your requirements will dictate your DAM application infrastructure. Some fundamental questions to ask:

- How many assets? How big are the assets?

- Who will be interacting with the application? Within the company? Suppliers? Internet customers?

- Where will these resources be located? Are there minimal throughput (file transfer) speeds that need to be met?

- Are there corporate audit requirements? Record retention? Archives? Rights auditing? Application back-up?

- Should my company host the application? Should I outsource? What are the security implications?

DAM ARCHITECTURE

The typical DAM architecture consists of four basic elements: a user interface, programming to process requests, a database, and a folder structure.

1. The user interface consists of the pages and forms that a DAM application user navigates to interact with the DAM.

2. Programming is the code that receives the request from the user, processes it, and returns appropriate results.

3. The database is part of the "back-end" of the application and stores all the metadata and user account data.

4. The folder structure is the other part of the back end, where the uploaded digital content is stored.

When a user requests a file for preview or download, a "call" is made from the "client" to the "server" where the program code runs; the code fetches a copy of the asset from the folder structure and the asset metadata from the database. This is the "traditional" design because assets stored *within* a database is a clunky operation. But as database management systems (DBMS) evolve, the storage of the asset in the database – as opposed to the folder structure – will become a reality (if it hasn't already). When evaluating DAM applications, request a high-level diagram of the architecture from the vendor.

The programming, folder, and database components – everything but the client -- could co-exist and execute on one computer (or "server"), but most architecture designs follow a three-tier format: client, web server, and database (the inclusion of the folder structure would necessitate a fourth tier), each reside on their own server. Obviously, the client will be whatever PC or MAC (or smartphone or tablet) the resource uses to access the DAM application. From there, a remote server hosts the application (web pages and programming logic), another server hosts the database (metadata and user account data), and another server hosts the file structure (which houses the actual digital assets). See figure below.

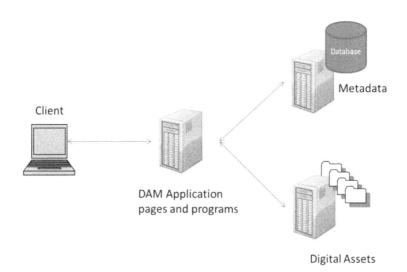

When a librarian performs an ingest, the digital file is moved to a predetermined location within the folder structure. There, the location (path) of the asset is transferred to the application which stores the path in the database. The rest of the asset metadata is stored along with the path in the database.

When a search is executed, the relevant metadata is returned from the database. If the user wants to see a preview, the thumbnail is clicked which sends a call to the file structure to retrieve the full asset for the preview. Likewise, when a download is requested, a copy of the file is made from the folder structure. Depending on the format, the file will be transferred as is or zipped (compressed) – either by itself or with other assets -- and then transferred to the user.

"Loosely coupling" the components make it easier to make upgrades and perform back-ups. For example, the version of the DAM programming can be upgraded without impacting the metadata or the digital files.

APPLICATION ENVIRONMENTS

If the expense of buying three different servers (one for each tier) wasn't costly enough, consider that this is only for the *production* environment. Large organizations usually have at least three environments, and occasionally more.

Typically, the three environments are:

- Development: This is where new versions of DAM software are deployed, existing bug fixes are tested, and new enhancements are introduced. The Development environment is sometimes called a "sandbox" as the purpose is simply to test programming changes before they are promoted to the production environment.

- Quality Assurance or "QA": The QA environment is a replica of the production environment; its function is to mirror how the change will look in a "pristine" production environment.

- Production: This is the environment where the actual users interact with the actual application. This is the environment that demands the most protection and attention.

CLIENT SOFTWARE (or CLIENT "LOAD" or CLIENT "CONFIG")

Client Configuration

Understanding the software required on the client or "user" side is critical. Ask the vendor what client (user) software is required to run the DAM application. If a company discovers that a particular version of external software is required (software other than the browser itself), the client instal-lation of this software may become an ordeal. So, the less software re-quired on the client side (none is ideal), the better.

Browser Compatibility

Another thing the company wants to ensure is that the DAM application can run on a variety of browsers. The DAM vendor may request that the company select one browser platform that is fully "certified" (that is, they will support use of their product for this specific browser), but the com-pany should ensure that at least two, and maybe three or four browsers are able to work without issue. Also, the company should ensure that browser *versions* are supported. A list of browsers and versions should be created, and then vendor-certified. Certification is basically testing to en-sure functions like searching, downloading, and viewing previews works consistently on each browser. It *is* in the best interests of the company to keep the deployment of browsers to a minimum (remember, when testing fixes and enhancements, each browser / browser version will have to be tested).

Example browser support list:

Browser	Version(s)
Edge	44, 46, 88
Internet Explorer	Not Supported
Safari	14
Chrome	87, 88
Firefox	78, 85

WHERE SHOULD THE DAM INFRASTRUCTURE BE? On-Premise, Cloud, or Software as a Service

The company purchasing a DAM has several options on how the application architecture is managed. There are three options:

1. Hosting a DAM within the company data center (On-premise)
2. Buying the software, but infrastructure hosting is in the cloud (Infrastructure as a Service, or IaaS)
3. Buying an application already in the cloud with no infrastructure investment (Software as a Service, or SaaS).

The third option, SaaS, allowing the vendor to manage the application and infrastructure is the trend now. It takes the least amount of time to stand up; the infrastructure is managed by the vendor, and communications between the DAM and other company-owned applications can be managed through Application Programming Interfaces (API's). SaaS solutions can integrate with your identity management systems (like Microsoft Active Directory).

However, strict security rules may force a company into managing its infrastructure.

The following table highlights advantages and disadvantages of a SaaS-based DAM. These options should be considered during the company's DAM application evaluation phase.

Feature	Options 1 and 2	Option 3
Deployment Period	Longer duration	Shorter duration
Hardware Administration / Sizing, back-ups, uptime	Need to provide	Included in price
Geographic support	Need to design, support, and administrate	Already designed into solution
Client configuration	Need to test, support multiple browsers	Already designed to accommodate popular browsers
Integration with security applications	Full	Limited

If the company is forced for security reasons into managing the DAM architecture, the following items should be reviewed.

HOSTING: Internal or External

Should the organization decide to host in the cloud, the DAM application vendor will likely recommend a hosting service that they trust. Usually, these cloud companies have proven global performance, robust availability (guaranteed uptime), and full back-up and security capability. The only downside of external hosting is the inability to integrate corporate security servers, meaning security policies may have to be written twice and additional logon ID's and passwords may be required. However, as more companies begin moving their services to the cloud, this becomes less of a hurdle; your company may have a cloud strategy that already addresses this issue.

On-premise Hosting

If security standards dictate that the DAM must be hosted WITHIN the company's data center, additional costs must be budgeted.

Additional Hardware: Often, large companies have servers to host each tier and each promotional environment, although other company applications may be served on shared servers. If your budget can afford it, it might be advisable to buy dedicated servers just for the DAM system; this gives you more control. Depending on the number of tiers in your architecture, you may want to consolidate some of the tiers on a single server (like the database and the folder structure).

Additional Software Licenses: Your vendor should provide you licenses for the Development and QA servers, as well as the production server, but they may charge you for them. Try to negotiate them in the package. Also, ask if any of the other components (like the database) require additional licensing as well. Also look to reduce annual maintenance charges on the additional license software: it might be free year one, but charges could be incurred after that.

Promotional Process: The deployment team should be aware of the process to promote a bug fix or an enhancement; in most large companies, several approvals are required to move the revisions through the promotion process. Also, revisions may not be able to be deployed immediately; company standards may require that updates to the production server be completed during scheduled maintenance (often, Sunday evenings, when usage is lowest).

STORAGE

It is often said nowadays that "storage is cheap". This may be an accurate description for storage itself, but back-up and other costs associated with the size of your asset folder will grow proportionately. One of the most efficient solutions is to keep data on a Storage Area Network or "SAN". These specially architected servers are designed to accommodate storage needs as the amount of data expands.

Deployment team members may meet resistance to a SaaS or IaaS cloud-based solution because it may not meet company security requirements. I would recommend that unless a requirement is totally irrefutable, that requirement should be re-written to accommodate the SaaS solution. Security is important, but it is often used as an excuse to *not* do something.

Unless the data is personal or highly confidential, the security of cloud-based DAM applications should be more than adequate.

COMMERCIAL or OPEN SOURCE

There are at least one-hundred vendors in the DAM space. Before embarking on evaluating a company solution, the organization may want to work with a consulting company, like Gartner or Forrester Research, to narrow the search for a vendor specifically to the nature of their organization and needs.

A list of current vendors is available here:

https://digitalassetmanagementnews.org/vendors/

Most of the products listed are **commercial**, meaning you pay for the software licenses. There are several **open-source** ("free") alternatives to commercial DAM applications. In fact, when evaluating the functionality of open source applications like *Resource Space (Montala Ltd)* and *Phraseanet (Alchemy)*, users will be surprised by the capability available. The open-source application is "free" in the sense that the application software itself is free. However, costs like customization, asset migration, hardware, and maintenance should be factored into the analysis, as well as costs like hosting and business support. There are "expert" hosting and maintenance companies experienced in supporting open-source solutions like Montala LTD for the *Resource Space* product, so don't exclude this alternative in your analysis.

PART 2: PLANNING FOR DEPLOYMENT

DEPLOYMENT PLANNING

Now the team is ready to initiate the deployment of a DAM application. Start with a high-level plan. The following are key activities that should be included in the plan:

1) Develop a charter to explain the business reasons why the DAM application should be deployed. The charter may include a budget and return-on-investment (ROI) analysis

2) Develop a high-level implementation schedule (Plan, develop requirements, perform product evaluation, refine requirements, do development work, test, and deploy)

3) Create a project team. This team should consist of stakeholders representing the various organizations that own digital assets as well as representatives from the internal support teams and the vendor (when the vendor comes on board)

4) Write a detailed project plan identifying known tasks

5) Develop business requirements: Identify the functionality required / available. This is an iterative process and requires some preliminary vendor evaluation to understand functionality that is available but may

not have been considered while writing the business requirements.

6) Define organizational fit: assign roles to actual resources (see next section)

7) Evaluate vendors

    i) Do research; contact consulting experts (like Gartner or Forrester)

    ii) Gather requirements, which DAM application functionality is required and which is optional

    iii) Evaluate commercial, cloud-based, and open-source solutions

    iv) Estimate costs

8) Select vendor

9) Develop or refine technical requirements. The vendor may be able to help you define / refine functional and technical requirements

10) Develop Asset Migration Plan (if required)

11) Procure software licenses / hardware (if required)

12) Develop User Rollout plan

13) Develop training plan

14) Install Hardware and Software

15) Begin development / customization

16) Write and Test Migration Scripts

17) Develop support processes

18) Migrate existing assets (if required)

19) Train

20) Perform User Acceptance Testing

21) Pilot

22) Fully deploy

DEPLOYMENT STRATEGY

The organization will likely progress in one of two ways: they will either develop requirements to accommodate several (or all) stakeholders in the organization, or they will concentrate on the needs of one team (perhaps the largest) and develop the DAM solution specifically for that team, with the intent of updating the application (if required) as each new set of digital asset owners comes on board.

As always, the approach is guided by a "business decision"; will the business reduce costs now by deploying quickly and therefore risk the inability of accommodating other asset / business needs later? Or will the business defer the cost savings with a less risky approach? Should the business follow a focused approach with less functionality or pursue an all-encompassing approach and risk becoming bloated?

Here are advantages and disadvantages of each approach (**bold** is better):

Activity	All-encompassing Approach	Targeted Approach
Time to market	Longer	**Shorter**
Risk of functional "bloat"	Higher	**Lower**
Risk of excluding needed functionality	**Lower**	Higher
Risk of "analysis paralysis"	Higher	**Lower**
Risk of System Bugs	Higher	**Lower**
DAM proof of capability / user "acceptance"	Longer	**Shorter**
Savings via DAM usage	Wait	**Now**

ORGANIZATIONAL ROLES

During the planning, it will be important to ensure that organizational roles exist or will need to be created to support the DAM application. The following is a short description of the departmental responsibilities for deployment and ongoing application support. When reviewing, the deployment team should understand who in the company will own these responsibilities.

Business Ownership

This is the individual / business team that owns the DAM application within the organization. Their responsibilities are:

- Budget the DAM application
- Create the deployment team
- Write the business requirements
- Determine organizational responsibility
- Work with internal stakeholders
- Identify (contract) business support
- Identify (contract) IT support
- Develop support processes
- Evaluate and select application and (optionally) host vendors
- Report on status
- Contract with the vendors
- Deploy the application

Business Ownership, Post-DAM deployment:
- Manage enhancements and upgrades
- Manage Business Support team
- Manage vendor support
- Manage the support processes
- Manage budget
- Maintain status

Business Support / Help Desk
- Respond to reported application defects (and downtime)
- Create / Modify / Delete user accounts
- Train
- Other administrative work

Librarians
- Ingest assets / add metadata

Information Technology
- Design network and infrastructure
- Procure and install hardware
- Monitor application uptime
- Perform back-ups and restores

DEVELOPING REQUIREMENTS

The foundation of any DAM application deployment is a solid set of requirements. The business team / project team is responsible for developing these requirements (and will likely work with the DAM application vendor to write technical and support process requirements).

The requirements can be classified into the following four categories:

- Business Requirements: Why is the business doing this?
- Functional Requirements: Which DAM features are required?
- Technical Requirements: How is this solution supported technically?
- Support Requirements: How is this solution supported organizationally?

Business Requirements: What are the business reasons for deploying a DAM application? What are the business requirements? Business requirements should be "technology agnostic"; that is, the requirements should not assume a technical solution but focus instead on the business requirements that need to be addressed.

The following examples are in abbreviated format. Your organization may have a template or process for documenting requirements. The goal is to ensure that all the requirements have been documented.

ID	Requirement	Reason	Test (this requirement will be successfully met when...)
1	Re-use digital assets	By re-using digital assets globally, the company can reduce asset creation costs by 20%. This will reduce costs by $x,xxx annually	Assets are re-used, and we can measure cost savings
2	Share assets across geographic regions	To share assets, we will need to enable our five global offices to partici-pate in sharing	Regional users can use assets created in other regions
3	Rights Protection	When sharing assets, us-ers must understand and comply with individual digital asset rights.	Users sharing assets un-derstand the rights as-sociated with the asset
4	Asset Security	We need to ensure that digital assets are used by the right markets for the right usage	Regional users are pro-hibited from sharing as-sets not yet released publicly, or not appro-priate for their market

Functional Requirements: At this point the company can assume that a DAM application will accommodate their business issues, and they will begin a more detailed description of the functionality required.

ID	Requirement	Reason	Test
25	Search by simple terms	Provide the user a method to locate the asset quickly by entering descriptive terms in a search box	The expectation of results based on a search term is returned to the user accurately
26	Search by specific metadata terms (advanced search)	Provide the user the ability to narrow their search by specifying values that correspond to metadata values	The expectation of results based on metadata value is returned to the user accurately
27	Search by tree method (drill down)	Provide the user the ability to search by starting at a specific root level (TBD), and selecting subsequent sub-levels, narrowing down the search	The expectation of results is returned accurately as the user drills further down from the root level
28	Search by asset content	Provide the user to search for assets by using content within the asset (like a word or a string of words)	The expectation of results from the content search is returned to the user accurately

Technical Requirements: These are the hardware / software / network requirements to support the functional requirements.

ID	Requirement	Reason	Test
229	Interface with company identity management system	Leverage existing user security database; eliminate need to create additional logon ID and password for internal users.	Internal users can logon with existing company logon ID and password
230	Achieve benchmark speeds for Asia and Africa offices	Ensure benchmark download speeds are achieved (50 MB file in less than 10 minutes)	Download tests are within benchmark parameters
231	System back-up requirements are met	Comply with audit requirements and ERP plans	Internal audit verifies back-up schedules are met
232	Adequate hardware support for three environments	Need to ensure that hardware for each environment is available	We have successfully promoted system deployment on all three environments (meets all UAT tests)

Process Requirements: The processes required to support the DAM Application.

ID	Requirement	Reason	Test
309	Account Request authorization	Need a process to define how users are authorized to access the application (access and role)	We can regularly authorize accounts in an organized, documented fashion
310	Environment Promotion approval	Need a process to determine how a software change is promoted from the Development environment to the QA environment, and from the QA environment to the Production environment	We can regularly promote fully tested software changes in an organized, documented fashion, and ensure that the production environment is not impacted negatively
311	Account Deletion	Need a process to delete unauthorized or dormant account ID's to comply with audit requirements	We can validate that the only ID's available in the application are authorized and up-to-date (on twice-yearly review dates)
312	User Bug Tracking	Need a process to track bugs reported by users	The business owner and application maintenance team can view and respond to all bugs reported

SUPPORT PROCESSES

The processes that support the application are as important as the application itself. Support processes should be developed and tested during the deployment phase. Some of the processes, like account creation, may exist.

Here is a list of the processes that should be developed and the concerns that the processes should address.

Business Processes

DAM Deployment and post-deployment status: Which stakeholders are interested in the status of the project deployment, process development, training plans, number of defects? How often do they meet? What do they need to know?

Reporting a Defect (from Support Team): How is a defect documented and tracked? What is the turn-around agreement with the vendor? How is it prioritized? Is this done via a spread sheet, a defect tracking tool? (for example, JIRA). How are defects prioritized?

Requesting an Enhancement (includes revising metadata) / Prioritizing Enhancements: If a resource (user or otherwise) has a suggestion for an improvement or an enhancement, how are these requests handled? How are they prioritized, budgeted, validated? Are they integrated into the maintenance process?

Enhancement Releases: Are enhancements deployed individually or bundled in a release? How are new releases tested and deployed?

Integrating a New Business Team / Asset Group: If new business teams want to begin storing their assets on the DAM application, how are they integrated? Will they need to provide budget?

Vendor Maintenance: What are the annual vendor costs? When are vendor costs prepared for budget? How are costs tracked? How are hours tracked? What are the annual business support costs? IT costs?

Vendor Support Processes

<u>Defect Fix:</u> What are the obligations for defect fix? How are defect fixes prioritized? How quickly must a defect fix be completed?

<u>Status:</u> How does the vendor report bug fixes or enhancements?

<u>Accounting:</u> How are support hours reported?

<u>Unit Testing:</u> How is unit testing performed, documented, approved?

<u>System Testing:</u> How is application testing performed, documented, approved?

Business Support (Help Desk) Processes

<u>Approving / Validating a User Account:</u> How does someone request an account? How is a request authorized? How is a user assigned a role?

<u>Creating a User Account:</u> Who creates the account? How is it documented? Is it created in an existing security application or within the DAM application itself? What is the turnaround (how many hours / days to create the account)?

<u>Deleting a User Account:</u> What are the criteria for deleting accounts (inactivity? unauthorized usage?) Can this process be automated? How is the deletion tracked?

<u>Reporting a Request / Defect (Bug) / Other (from user):</u> How are user requests tracked? Are they documented? Can they be reported on?

<u>User Acceptance Testing:</u> How is UAT organized? Who writes the test plan? What roles need to be tested? What functionality needs to be tested?

<u>Training:</u> Training plans / Training schedules; who needs training? When will it be scheduled? In what format? Real-time (Zoom/ TEAMS), Videos?

Librarian Processes

<u>Ingesting Assets / Adding metadata:</u> What is the process for ingesting assets? What is the metadata add / modify policy? Are requests captured on a user form? Are requests logged?

Rules Processes

Archiving Assets: Does the organization have any documented record retention or audit requirements? When does an asset become inactive or archived; when is it deleted?

Deleting Assets: What are the criteria for asset deletion? Are deletions tracked? Do the assets remain in the folder structure / database?

Watermarking Assets: What criteria are used to watermark an asset? Are assets tracked (with tools like Digimarc, PicScout); is every asset tracked?

Rights Usage: How are rights enforced on assets? By what metadata criteria? Are alerts required during download; are there special prohibitions?

IT Processes (applies ONLY to companies managing DAM infrastructure)

Promoting fixes / enhancements to the Production Environment: What is the process for promoting enhancements and fixes from the development environment to the QA environment to the production environment? How are promotions and fixes "undone"; demoted? What approvals are required?

IT Support: How is IT support contacted? What is the process? What criteria must be met? Is it manually or via a system? What is the turnaround support time / under what circumstances?

Maintenance Window: What is the window for maintenance; weekly? What items are performed? How is it backed-out?

Back-up Process: How often is the application backed-up? Where are files stored offsite? Who has written the Disaster Recovery Plan or Emergency Resource Plan (how quickly will the application be back online if the hardware is suddenly damaged or inaccessible?)

USER ROLL-OUT PLAN

A user roll-out plan describes when and how the DAM application is deployed to users. The plan should include the following activities and should be integrated in the master project schedule:

1) <u>List of Users</u>: Identify which users will be on-boarded and when. The team needs to determine if they want to release the DAM application to all users at once or release it in phases. User ID's will need to be created.

2) <u>Training Plan:</u> Begin developing a training plan, if required. The goal for DAM application vendors is to make the experience as intuitive and user-friendly as possible, so that training costs are minimized. (Remember, websites like eBay and Amazon don't train their users!) Instructions and help screens should be easy to access and, ideally, context sensitive (If you are ingesting assets, the help available should recognize that you are on the ingest page and should offer help on the ingest function). The company may also consider producing videos which describe the most common functions of the application.

3) <u>User Notification:</u> The team needs to create an awareness of the deployment and publish the schedule to users and stakeholders. At this point, you may also be soliciting user interest and / or ID information to create accounts. If asking for user information, be prepared: geographic markets have different personal information requirements. The users need to know things like the website URL and Business Support contact information.

4) <u>User Accounts Creation:</u> Using your account creation process, begin creating user ID's. You may want to hold on to these until the user is scheduled for application access. By this time, you should have a process established for determining how you assign access roles.

5) <u>Training:</u> Begin executing the training that you developed in the previous phase.

6) <u>User Acceptance Testing</u> (on DAM application and supporting processes): Before being rolled-out to users, the DAM application must be fully user tested. User testing describes the testing of the functionality defined in the requirements document. Adequate time must be allocated for testing; there are bound to be defects, and the effort to fix a

defect may be considerable. To launch without any defects is ideal, but improbable, so as the first launch or pilot draws near, there will have to be decisions made regarding whether to launch based on the number and impact of defects. Rule of thumb, if the major functions are impacted (search, results and download), the launch should be delayed. If the defect impacts an optional function (like Zoom In), the team may launch and resolve the issue later.

7) Business Support (Help Desk) Team in place: Before the first users access the system, the Business Support Team must be put in place, ready to execute tested processes.

8) Pilot the launch to a small group of users

9) Gradually launch by (some category)/ Launch to all users

10) Monitor usage

ASSET MIGRATION

The company may already have a DAM application, or they don't have an application and will likely be moving assets from a company share drive (or drives). In any case, a migration plan must be developed.

Moving from an Existing DAM Application

Companies that currently use a DAM application to store assets have a slight advantage (if they have the access to the database to pull the information required) and can migrate by mapping existing metadata to the new metadata fields. Not every field will map one-to-one, and some field sizes may be different. If using commercial software, the new vendor is likely to assist in the migration.

On the next page is a sample migration map: The current DAM application fields are in the *Source Metadata Field* column, the new fields in the *Target Metadata Field* column.

For example, in the first row, we map the data in the current metadata field *System ID* to the new DAM application field *Identifier*. But in this case, the business team has decided not to copy the data over. A new number will be pulled from the system during the migration, per the approach instructions, and populate the *Target Metadata field*. (If the company wants to retain the *SystemID* from the previous DAM application, they can create a field in the new DAM – for example, *Former System ID* -- and move the old *SystemID* value into that new field).

Source Metadata Field	Target Field	Approach
System ID	Identifier	Ignore System ID, Identifier will be new and assigned during migration upload
Subject	Subject	Move
Description	Description	Move
	Location	New field; will be blank
Color	Color	Moving to shorter field; will truncate last 4 characters. Identify all assets with longer color names, and mass update with abbreviated version prior to migration
	Resolution Options	New field; will be blank
Status	Asset Status	Move
	Restricted Users	New field; will be blank
File	File Name	Ignore; will pull from system data
	Rights Associated	New field; will be blank
	Rights Expiry Date	New field; will be blank
	Rights Media Usage	New field; will be blank
	Rights Market Usage	New field; will be blank
Name	Title	Move
	Price	New field; will be blank
Keywords	Keywords	Move
	Type	New field; will pull automatically at migration
	Video Type	New field; will be blank
	Format	New field; will pull automatically at migration
Librarian	Publisher	Move
Date Uploaded	Date Ingested	Move
	Photographer	New field; will pull automatically at migration
	Size	New field; will pull automatically at migration
Program		Not migrating
Program Sponsor		Not migrating

Migration Testing and Timing

The date for the migration of assets will need to be planned. On a specified date (known as the "cut-off date"), users will have to stop ingesting in the current application. There may be some time lapse (perhaps a week or two), before they can begin ingesting in the new application (called an ingest "freeze"). Between these dates, the migration activity from old system to new system takes place. On the cut-off date, the known list of assets to be migrated is confirmed, and access to the old system is disabled. Special "scripts" are run to move metadata from the old system database to the new system database, and to move the assets to the new folder structure. Extensive testing is executed to ensure the expected data is now present in the new system.

There is no harm in copying and moving metadata for *testing* much earlier than the cut-off date. In fact, the earlier this is done, the better.

No Existing DAM Application

This migration may be a much bigger challenge. The team will need to determine which assets will move to the DAM application and which ones will not.

For existing assets residing on share drives or user computers, little information other than file and folder properties may be available. A strategy needs to be developed to determine how the metadata fields for these assets are populated. The organization may opt to move the assets into the new application manually, as if they were new assets, or they may decide to move them via an ingest script written by the DAM application vendor.

To obtain some very simple metadata, the asset's file path can be "parsed". "Parsing" means slicing up the path name by folder and using the folder names as metadata.

Here is an example:

T:\ABC Program\Exterior\Williams\sunflower.tif

In this example, the digital asset "sunflower.tif" exists in a sub-folder named *Williams* (named for the photographer), within a sub-folder named *Exterior*, within a folder named *ABC program*.

A spreadsheet can "parse" the path (cut it up) using the "\" symbol, and produce the following metadata:

Program   ABC Program

Location   Exterior

Photographer Williams

Title   sunflower

As there is no *program* metadata field in the new system, the first field can be ignored. The second item (*Location*) can be moved to the new *location* field. The third field (*photographer*) can be moved to the *photographer* field. The fourth field (which is the parsed first piece of the file name – the part before the file extension; in this example, *sunflower*) can be moved to the *Title* field.

Here is the issue: it is highly unlikely that your digital assets currently exist in a set folder path pattern. It's more likely the path patterns vary widely for each group of digital assets. The company has two options: they can parse and migrate in groups of assets (parsing each path individually), or they can move the assets to a pre-determined file path within the folder structure and then parse and migrate the assets from this new folder structure. The vendor may provide scripts to load this parsed data, so the first option may not be too difficult.

On the next few pages, we provide an example of how a file path could be parsed to create metadata.

In this example, asset file paths are parsed using Excel (we have added the heading and the ID field). The parsed data will then end up as metadata field values in the target DAM application. For example, the data may look like this after parsing:

ID	Program	Location	Photographer	Title	Extension	Date Taken	Price
1	ABC Program	Exterior	Williams	sunflower	tif		
2	ABC Program	Exterior	Williams	sunflower2	tif		
3	ABC Program	Exterior	Williams	sunflower3	tif		
4	ABC Program	Exterior	Williams	roses	tif		
5	ABC Program	Exterior	Williams	roses2	tif		
6	ABC Program	Exterior	Williams	lily2	tif		
7	ABC Program	Exterior	Williams	lily4	tif		
8	ABC Program	Interior	Williams	cactus1	tif		
9	ABC Program	Interior	Williams	cactus4	tif		
10	CDE Program	Exterior	Smith	cactus texasa	jpg		
11	CDE Program	Exterior	Smith	cactus texasb	jpg		
12	CDE Program	Exterior	Smith	cactus texasc	jpg		
13	CDE Program	Interior	Bailey	redrose40	tif		
14	CDE Program	Interior	Bailey	redrose82	tif		
15	ABC Program	Allen	Interior Shots	New York	2024	A127HxA	
16	ABC Program	Allen	Interior Shots	New York	2025	A12VCDHxA	
17	ABC Program	Allen	Interior Shots	New jersey	2025	A127Lbb1	
18	ABC Program	Allen	Interior Shots	New Jersey	2025	A127Lbb2	
19	Ext	2025	Apple Tree.png	Image	Vermont	402	1200.00
20	Ext	2025	Apple Tree 1.png	Image	Vermont	402	1200.00
21	Ext	2025	Apple Tree 2.png	Image	New Hampshire	387	980.00

The parsing strategy works fine for assets 1 to 14. However, new fields will have to be defined, and further parsing will need to be done to process records 15 through 21   Also note, the filenames in records 15 through 18 are cryptic; the migration team may decide to keep the filename as the title or overwrite the title manually.

With some additional cut and paste activity, the company can retrofit the last seven records (and however many more variations are found). Obviously, if the data doesn't exist in the file path, there is nothing to move into these fields. For example, in records 19 through 21 below, the *program* and the *photographer* are not present in the file path.

ID	Program	Location	Photographer	Title	Extension	Date Taken	Price
1	ABC Program	Exterior	Williams	sunflower	tif		
2	ABC Program	Exterior	Williams	sunflower2	tif		
3	ABC Program	Exterior	Williams	sunflower3	tif		
4	ABC Program	Exterior	Williams	roses	tif		
5	ABC Program	Exterior	Williams	roses2	tif		
6	ABC Program	Exterior	Williams	lily2	tif		
7	ABC Program	Exterior	Williams	lily4	tif		
8	ABC Program	Interior	Williams	cactus1	tif		
9	ABC Program	Interior	Williams	cactus4	tif		
10	CDE Program	Exterior	Smith	cactus texasa	jpg		
11	CDE Program	Exterior	Smith	cactus texasb	jpg		
12	CDE Program	Exterior	Smith	cactus texasc	jpg		
13	CDE Program	Interior	Bailey	redrose40	tif		
14	CDE Program	Interior	Bailey	redrose82	tif		
15	ABC Program	Interior	Allen	A127HxA		2024	
16	ABC Program	Interior	Allen	A12VCDHxA		2025	
17	ABC Program	Interior	Allen	A127Lbb1		2025	
18	ABC Program	Interior	Allen	A127Lbb2		2025	
19		Exterior		Apple Tree	png	2025	1200.00
20		Exterior		Apple Tree 1	png	2025	1200.00
21		Exterior		Apple Tree 2	png	2025	980.00

Other migration considerations:

- Put the path name as the metadata *title* or *description*. It may not explain much, but it's better than nothing, and much easier to execute than parsing file paths.

- Open the DAM application up to new assets only. "Beginning January 2024, all new digital assets will be stored in the new DAM application."

- Some metadata field, perhaps *publisher*, should reflect that this is a migrated asset.

- Ingest the assets but keep them in "private" status where only selected users can view, add metadata, and eventually make the assets available to other users.

File Names

Two other items to consider:

- Although DAM applications allow assets to share a *title* within the application, duplicate file names are usually not allowed. This may require re-naming files before posting.

- Also check to understand how many file name characters are allowed. Some DAM applications have limitations to the number of characters within the file name; ensure that file names aren't too long.

TESTING

Adequate testing time must be scheduled into the project plan throughout the course of the deployment. The company and the vendor working together will perform Unit testing, System testing, Load testing, and Network testing. Here is a list of the testing (minimally) that will need to occur:

Test Type	Description	Responsible	Phase	Tool
Unit	Functionality is tested as code is developed	Programmer / Vendor	Development	Vendor internal process
System	"Units" are aggregated and tested as an integrated whole	Programmer / Vendor	Development	Vendor internal process
Network	Downloading and uploading speeds are tested according to targets set for each market	User / Vendor	Pre-user Acceptance Testing	Network targets
Load	Determine how many users can access the system concurrently before system performance is degraded	Vendor	Pre-user acceptance testing	Load targets
User Acceptance (Regression)	Actual application users test system functionality	User / Vendor	User Acceptance Testing	Test Plan

When to Test

Although testing will be done prior to DAM application deployment, testing will be done *after* deployment as well, particularly when fundamental changes are deployed or when a new release is installed. When a new version of the software is launched, users run through the test plan from beginning to end; this is called **regression testing**. Regression testing ensures that new functionality doesn't accidentally break existing functionality.

Environment (for companies managing the DAM infrastructure)

The users will perform testing within the environments in succession. Testing will begin within the development environment, proceed to the QA environment, and, when all tests are passed and functionality is "signed-off" (approved by the business owner), move to the production environment (where it should again be tested).

User Acceptance Testing (UAT)

When doing user acceptance testing, the test plan should be distributed to actual users, or resources simulating other users, ensuring that all role and market functionality is tested. Some companies have the luxury of a testing team. This team should be involved in the planning at the very beginning to understand how the application works.

Preparing the UAT

Using our role matrix, all the roles listed should be tested to ensure that the appropriate functionality does (or doesn't) work. In this scenario, there would be at least four roles doing the testing, each role validating that functionality works as documented. For example, the testing should validate that the Read and Download (RD) role can download assets and should *also* validate that the RD role *cannot* ingest assets.

Role	Read	Down-load	Ingest	Make Pri-vate	Private Read	Delete
Read (R)	X					
Read and Download (RD)	X	X				
Read, Download, and Ingest (RDI)	X	X	X	X		
Administrator (A)	X	X	X	X	X	X

Developing a Schedule / Notifying the Testers

UAT takes place after development and before deployment. Depending on the size of the test plan, an estimate for the testing period is determined (or the timing from the original project plan is validated). If the amount of testing that needs to be done requires many testers, these resources must be identified as quickly as possible. Testers are given test plans and roles to test before the UAT period begins. At least one orientation meeting should be held to review the test plan and discuss the process for reporting defects. Frequent (probably daily) meetings to gather information on defects are scheduled in advance.

Creating a Test Plan

In this example, we have created a test plan by modifying the requirements document and converting every functional requirement into a test. The test plan will include more information than the requirements document to test the many possible user scenarios. This plan tests functionality by role. If the user is testing the RDI role, they would record their results in the column labeled *RDI*:

ID	Require-ment	Test Process	Result	R	RD	RDI	A
25.1	Search by simple terms	Enter the term "sunflower" in the simple search box, then click sub-mit	Data will return "sunflower" images, includ-ing those with the term in these metadata fields: File name Subject Title Keywords				
25.2	Search by simple term sub-string	Enter the term "flower" in the simple search box, then click submit	Should receive the same re-sults as previ-ous test				
25.3	Simple Search "and" test	Enter the term "sunflower" and "exterior" with a space in between the two terms	Should receive results from 25.2, but only those that also have "exterior" in a metadata field				
25.4	Simple Search "all" test	Enter an aster-isk "*", then click submit	Max results (all viewable as-sets) should be returned to user				

When the test plan is complete, it will be distributed to the testers. The UAT will begin on a specific date, and meetings to report defects should commence.

Data for Testing

Note that there are "expected results". The results are based on the test data available in the system. Either the test plan will determine how this data will be prepared, or the data available will determine the expected results in the test plan. In any event, a set of digital assets needs to be prepared for testing. Ideally, this would be a copy of the current set of assets the organization already has in its DAM application, or, if no application, a set of representative assets. The more "production-like" the test data, the better. It would also be ideal to test every possible format of asset as well, in a variety of sizes, ensuring that the thumbnail and preview capability work as required. Depending on how your IT department is organized, you will need to identify the resource that will assist in preparing this data. It will likely be the same resource assisting with your migration activity.

Here is an example of how the test plan may be completed by someone testing the RDI role:

ID	Require-ment	Test Pro-cess	Result	R	RD	RDI	A	Other
25.1	Search by simple terms	Enter the term "sun-flower" in the simple search box, then click submit	Data will re-turn "sun-flower" im-ages, includ-ing those with the term in these metadata fields: File name Subject Title Keywords			Passed		
25.2	Search by simple term substring	Enter the term "flower" in the simple search box, then click submit	Should re-ceive the same re-sults as pre-vious test			Passed		
25.3	Simple Search "and" test	Enter the term "sun-flower" and "exterior" with a space in be-tween the two terms	Should re-ceive results from 25.2, but only those that also have "exterior" in a metadata field			Passed		
25.4	Simple Search "all" test	Enter an as-terisk "*", then click submit	Max results (all viewable assets) should be returned to user			Fail: re-ceived no re-sults		

Note that the first three tests passed, but the fourth failed. In this test, the asterisk -- known as a "wildcard" -- was supposed to return every asset viewable by that role. However, during test it failed to return any assets. Depending on how often the team meets, this defect needs to be forwarded to the project team, prioritized, and fixed.

Usually during UAT, there are frequent meetings where test results are reviewed with the users and the vendor. At these meetings, defects are reported, priorities assigned, and progress on fixing the defect is shared. Some companies may utilize defect reporting software (for example, Jira) for logging the defects; other companies may use a simple spreadsheet. Here is an example of a defect reporting spreadsheet:

ID	Priority	Description	Date	Reported by	Comments / Screen Prints	Assigned to	Status	Target Date
28	1	"A" role can't download non-market assets (38.14)	5/10/2025	Jones		Vendor	In process	5/12/2025
12	2	"A" video download issue (129.2)	5/4/2025	Williams		Vendor	In process	5/13/2025
2	3	Private asset functionality not working for RDI role (98.1)	5/3/2025	Jones	See screen print	Jones	Testing Fix	5/12/2025
3	4	Wildcard returning no results (25.4)	5/2/2025	Smith	Ask Smith to retest	Vendor	Not started	
17	5	.jpg conversion functionality not working (201.14)	5/5/2025	Baker	Conversion functionality working for all other formats	Vendor	In process	5/15/2025
35	6	.indd files not displaying (194.31)	5/12/2025	Vendor		Vendor	Not started	

This log includes a description of the defect including a reference to the test plan ID, the date reported, who reported it, additional comments (and perhaps a copy of a screen print), who the defect is assigned to for resolution, and the target date for completion.

In this example, the defects are ordered in the priority determined by the business team. The vendor will execute the fixes in the priority order assigned.

Network Testing

The organization should set acceptable throughput speed standards for ingesting and downloading digital assets in all regional locations. For example, the company may determine that a 60 MB file must finish downloading within ten minutes. This is a critical issue for companies that are deploying globally; the company needs to understand that internet infrastructure in developing markets may not be as robust as in mature markets. If the application is be used by external companies, these standards should apply to (and should be tested by) users at the external locations as well.

Here are sample target network speed plans:

TARGET

s=seconds	Region A		Region E		Region F		Region G	
	Ingest	Download	Ingest	Download	Ingest	Download	Ingest	Download
100 KB	40 S	30 S	50 S	50 S	120 S	90 S	130 S	100 S
10 MB	300 S	200 S	330 S	220 S	600 S	400 S	800 S	600 S
60 MB	600 S	500 S	660 S	550 S	3500 S	1200 S	4000 S	2400 S
250 MB	1200 S	800 S	1400 S	1000 S	4500 S	1500 S	6000 S	3200 S
1 GB	2000 S	1500 S	2400 S	1800 S				
2 GB	3500 S	2500 S	4000 S	3000 S				

The company may accept various speeds in different markets or take steps to improve throughput. Sometimes the company may be able to tweak the network, or add network equipment, to boost the speed. A "firewall-friendly" technology called UDP can speed transfer times dramatically.
The company may want to define acceptable speeds for their markets prior to test. The project team should work with their network team to agree what these standards should be.

Load Testing

Load testing determines how well the system can handle the processing load (amount of activity) based on concurrent user activity.

To prepare, the company estimates how many users will be on the system:

Region / Timeframe	Users	Logged On	Concurrent
Region A peak	250	15	5
Region A off-peak	250	5	2
Region E peak	200	15	4
Region E off-peak	200	4	2
Region F peak	140	10	3
Region F off-peak	140	2	1
Region G peak	90	5	1
Region G off-peak	90	2	1

The matrix says that in Region A, there are 250 users. This means that there are 250 user id's in Region A, capable of logging on to the application. During peak usage hours (probably 9:00 a.m. to 4:00 p.m. weekdays), the team expects there to be 15 users logged on to the system at any point in time, but not necessarily active in it. (Think of your email client; you are logged on all day, but only use it a certain percentage of the time). Of the 15 users logged on, five will be active, which means they are concurrently searching for, ingesting or downloading assets.

The vendor (probably working with your IT team) must test the processing server to ensure that five users can use the system concurrently without causing performance degradation.

Appendix: Calculating a Return on Investment (ROI)

Before deploying a DAM system, stakeholders should develop Return on Investment (ROI) metrics to justify costs. Cost savings and cost avoidance should be calculated to determine if a DAM solution is worthwhile.

Let's review the reasons why an organization would deploy a DAM:

Re-use

Leverage existing digital assets so that new assets do not need to be produced.

Self-service

Provide a user-friendly platform for users to search, review, and download assets, so that support resources are not necessary.

Brand Enforcement

Restrict access to ensure that those assets available for distribution align with the company's branding guidelines.

Security

Restrict access so that the assets available are only those authorized by the company for distribution.

Business Insights

Provide insights regarding asset usage and overall marketing strategy.

Each of these features provides opportunities for cost savings and cost avoidance. Companies can refine the formulas presented to develop an ROI relevant to their business.

Re-use

The ability to re-use assets for various marketing purposes significantly decreases costs. For a global company, asset re-use reduces the need for external markets to produce their own assets; markets spend a fraction of original production costs by customizing existing assets.

A simple formula can be created to calculate savings. An assumption can be made that costs to produce a new asset are eliminated for every x number of images downloaded. A simple survey can be distributed, asking asset users how often they customize existing assets versus producing them from scratch. For example, a company may determine that for every two hundred images downloaded, the production of a new asset is avoided.

Savings can be calculated as follows:

- Total number of images downloaded: a
- Number of downloaded images that replace a new production: b
- Average cost of producing an asset: c

Therefore,

(a/b) * c = cost savings

Example: 1,000 images were downloaded (a). It is determined that for every two hundred images downloaded, the company eliminates the need to produce a new asset (b). The production cost of a new asset is $10,000 (c):

(1000/200) * $10,000 = $50,000

Although a DAM is not required for asset re-use, it simplifies the process of distribution and selection. Therefore, the company might further refine the cost savings to show that post-DAM deployment improved asset re-use capability by x percent. So, assuming 20% re-use capability, the revised savings for using the DAM would be:

20% * $50,000 (total re-use savings) = $10,000

Self-service

Companies that do not use a DAM system are likely to store re-usable assets in a mass storage application like Dropbox, Box, or Google Drive. Users navigating these applications have limited search and review capabilities. As such, these storage approaches often force users to contact support personnel for assistance in locating the assets they need.

We can assume that the complexity of locating assets is a function of the number of assets made available by the company. For companies that distribute a small amount of assets, say one hundred or less, this is not an issue. But for companies offering thousands or tens of thousands of assets, users can quickly get lost trying to locate what they need.

The company can formulate a savings function based on the number of assets they make available.

Let us assume that for every 1,000 assets stored in a mass storage application, 15 minutes of user support is required per day.

Our savings formula:

- Number of assets available for download: a
- Number of assets that require user support: b
- Hourly amount of time required per day: c
- Hourly cost for support resource: d
- Support days per year: e

Therefore,

$(a/b) * c * d * e = \text{cost savings}$

Example: The company makes 5,000 assets available for download (a). It is determined that for every 1,000 images available, a support resource is required to assist users locating specific assets (b). The support resource spends fifteen minutes on average assisting users (c). The hourly resource cost is $25 (d). Number of support days per year is 200 (e).

$(5000/1000) * .25$ (15 minutes, or 25% of an hour) $* \$25 * 200 = \$6,250$ annual savings

Brand Enforcement and Security
DAM systems ensure that partners can access only the assets that conform to the brand guidelines defined by the company.

Although it would be difficult to quantify savings based on brand conformity, companies recognize that assets that do not conform present a deviation from the company's current marketing strategy. This can trigger unexpected costs for the company; marketing material created with digital assets that do not follow branding guidelines must be located, retrieved, and corrected.

DAM systems also ensure that partners can only access the assets that the company wants to make available. Secure assets are often shared within the DAM for collaborative purposes. Unintended access to these assets could result in unexpected costs, confusion, or embarrassment.
The company may state that brand enforcement and asset security can be represented in a specific dollar amount in cost avoidance. It may be better simply to state the DAM acts as an "insurance policy," protecting the company from costs that result from resolving brand enforcement and asset security issues.

If the company has experienced an actual setback because of one or both issues, it would be beneficial to demonstrate how those issues could have been avoided by using a DAM.

Business Insights

A DAM system can inform a company about marketing trends. DAM support teams regularly run statistics on number of users, number of downloads, user issues, and other valuable information. These statistics can provide analytical insight along these dimensions:

Asset content:

Which assets are being downloaded most frequently? Does this align to business expectations, or is the company encountering anomalies? For example, the company may be expecting that a certain set of assets would be widely downloaded and distributed because of a new advertising campaign. Is this happening? What other trends can be detected by examining the assets that users are actually downloading?

Geographic location of users:

Where are the downloads taking place? Are there regions that are doing more (or less) downloading than other regions? Are regions producing new assets that could be re-used by other regions?

Downloader roles and affiliations:

Who is doing the downloading? Users within the company? Agency users? Which agency is doing the most downloading? Should we be expecting other agencies to do more downloading?

Again, these insights may be difficult to quantify from a cost perspective. However, any insight that causes a company to change direction or adopt a new strategy can have a significant impact on costs. A statement reflecting that should be presented as part of regular cost savings reporting.

About the author
Ed Engman is a project manager with over 25 years of experience in the field of Information Technology. Over the past several years, Ed has been involved in the deployment or management of multiple digital asset management applications. Ed has an undergraduate degree in Economics from Oakland University in Rochester, Michigan, and received his MBA from Wayne State University in Detroit. He has also been teaching Business Systems at the community college level since 1996. Ed received PMI certification in 2002.

Ed is currently employed as a consultant for Hart Talbot. He and his family live in the Detroit area.

About Hart Talbot
Hart Talbot is a consulting firm specializing in the deployment of Digital Asset Management systems. Our consultants work with clients to evaluate, deploy, and manage these systems.

The Hart Talbot web page can be found at:

www.harttalbot.com

INDEX

www.ingramcontent.com/pod-product-compliance
Lightning Source LLC
LaVergne TN
LVHW051710050326
832903LV00032B/4128